ASTONISHING FACTS

Your hands and feet developed from the **fish's fin**.

Woolly mammoths **moulted** in summer, losing all their long hair, only keeping a coat **about one inch** long.

The earliest camels did **not** have humps.

AMAZING FACTS about PREHISTORIC ANIMALS

Illustrated by BOBBIE CRAIG

Opossums are hardly any different now than they were **90 million** years ago.

The **largest** dinosaur eggs were found in southern France. They could probably hold **3.5 quarts** and are thought to be as big as a reptile's egg can grow. A larger egg would need a thicker shell and be difficult for the baby to break through.

A fossilized dinosaur skull may weigh over **1 ton**, as heavy as a **motor cycle**.

The **largest** animal that has **ever** lived is the **blue whale**. It weighs the same as **4** of the dinosaur called Apatosaurus, which was one of the **heaviest** prehistoric animals that ever lived.

253 gastroliths (stomach stones used to digest food) weighing **17.95 pounds** were found in a marine reptile in the U.S.A.

Trilobites, sea-dwelling animals, developed large, round eyes with over **1000** lenses.

Worms, **500 million** years old, have been found whose tiny jaws can **still** be opened and shut.

A Moscow museum has a dinosaur claw **28 inches** along the curve – probably **longer than your arm!**

In 1784 a writer thought the Pterosaur's wings were **fins** and that it lived in the **sea**.

HOW TALL,

COPSOGNATHUS

AS TALL AS ...
= 8 inches =

A HEN

HYRACOTHERIUM
(EARLY HORSE)

AS TALL AS ...

A FOX

= 1 foot =

MOERITHERIUM (EARLY PIG)

AS TALL AS ...
**3 feet
= 4 inches =**

A LARGE PIG

DIATRYMA
(MONSTER BIRD)

AN AFRICAN ELEPHANT

AS TALL AS ...
**= 9 feet =
10 inches**

AS TALL AS ...
**= 19 feet =
8 inches**

TYRANNOSAURUS

A GIRAFFE

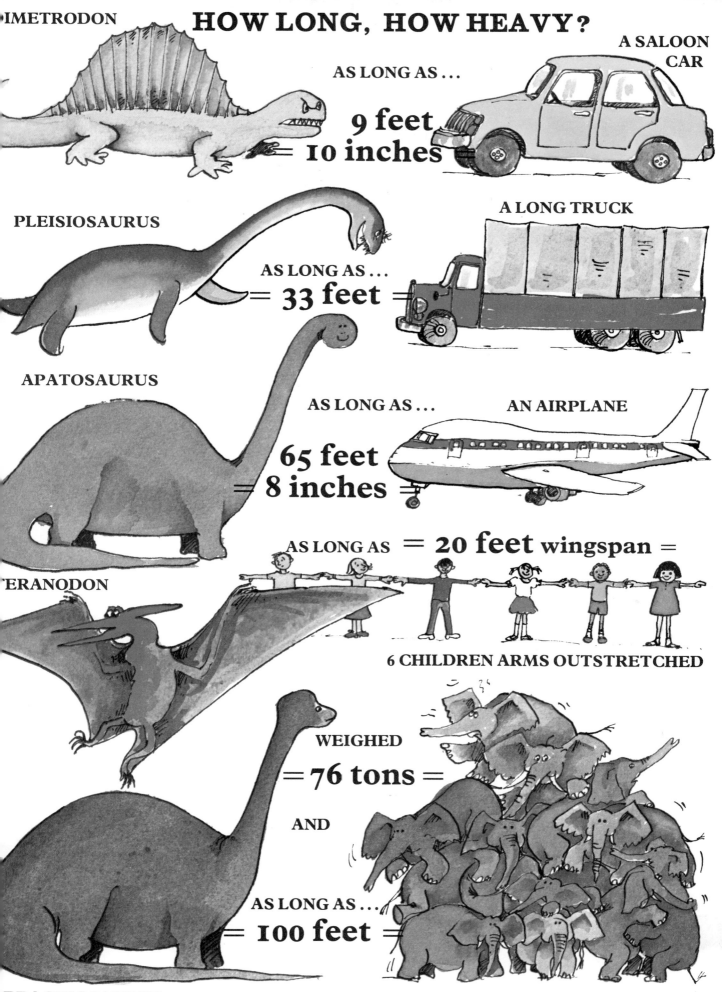

HOW LONG, HOW HEAVY?

IMETRODON

A SALOON CAR

AS LONG AS ...

9 feet = 10 inches

PLEISIOSAURUS

A LONG TRUCK

AS LONG AS ... **= 33 feet =**

APATOSAURUS

AS LONG AS ... AN AIRPLANE

65 feet = 8 inches =

AS LONG AS **= 20 feet** wingspan =

ERANODON

6 CHILDREN ARMS OUTSTRETCHED

WEIGHED **= 76 tons =**

AND

AS LONG AS ... **= 100 feet =**

BRACHIOSAURUS

12 ELEPHANTS

TIME SCALE SHOWING HOW LIFE DEVELOPED

NAME OF PERIOD	LENGTH OF TIME	LIFE EXISTING THEN
1 HOLOCENE	10 thousand years ago	Modern man. Domestic animals.
2 PLEISTOCENE	1 million years ago	Early man. Ice Age mammals – Mammoth; Woolly Rhin More modern camel. Glyptodon, then modern Armadillo Flesh-eating mammals – Puma; Sabre-toothed tiger. Ice Ages – Ice covers most of Europe, America and Anta
3 PLIOCENE	11 million years ago	Early Horse and other grass-eaters. Some mammals become too large. Giant Rhinoceros. Lands and seas begin to look more like those of today.
4 MIOCENE	25 million years ago	Camel becoming bigger. Early Apes. Modern Crabs, Snails. True mammals flourished – Sheep; Goats; Cows; Early Horse.
5 OLIGOCENE	40 million years ago	Early pig-sized Elephants. Early rabbit-sized Camels. Many flowering plants, seeds, fruit, vegetables. Seas retreat and the Alps beginning to form.
6 EOCENE	58 million years ago	Beginning of Early Horse. Mammals developing. Reptiles still surviving – Crocodiles, Turtles, Snakes, L Early marsupials. Mountains continue to develop. Seas cover areas of Europe. Formation of Atlantic and
7 PALEOCENE	65 million years ago	In-between mammals – Platypus; Echidna. End of dinosaurs.
8 CRETACEOUS	135 million years ago	Flowering plants. Bees, Crickets, Grasshoppers. Dinosaurs dominate the land. Fish develop in the sea. Formation of the chalk cliffs – Dover, Dorset, N. Ame Canada. Beginnings of the Rockies, the Andes and Eu
9 JURASSIC	180 million years ago	First birds – Archaeopteryx. Dinosaurs becoming larger and fiercer. Flying dinosaurs. Mammals still small, living in trees, burrows, etc.
10 TRIASSIC	225 million years ago	First mammals evolve from reptiles. In the sea fierce First dinosaurs, very small. First reptiles, early ancestors of Crocodiles, Turtles, Lizards, Snakes and Tuatara.
11 PERMIAN	270 million years ago	Early amphibians, ancestors of – Frogs, Toads, Newts Winged insects – Dragonflies. Formation of high mountains in Europe and America.
12 CARBONIFEROUS	350 million years ago	Fish begin to leave the water – Lungfish. Trees become much bigger. Climate hot and moist.
13 DEVONIAN	400 million years ago	Cockroaches. Small fish leave sea to live on the land. Early Spiders. Land plants develop. Cephalopods. Fish grow bigger, more aggressive and dominate the se Considerable volcanic activity, mountains beginning t
14 SILURIAN	440 million years ago	First plants on land. Scorpions in the sea No animals live on land. Fish develop in size
15 ORDOVICIAN	500 million years ago	Very early primitive fish. First sea creatures with back-bones. No life on land. Corals. Sea Urchins; Lobsters.
16 CAMBRIAN	600 million years ago	Sponges; Jellyfish; Starfish; Cephalopods. Microscopic creatures. Seaweeds; Sea-lilies; Sea anemonies; Worms.
17 PRE-CAMBRIAN		No life on the land or in the sea.

TIME CLOCK

MAN (1)

GENOZOIC
(Periods 2-7)

MESOZOIC
(Periods 8-10)

PALAEOZOIC
(Periods 11-16)

PROTEROZOIC
(Period 17)

AZOIC
(NO LIFE)

Trying to imagine time stretching back for thousands of millions of years is almost impossible. If you picture all of geological time on the face of a clock you will see that life has existed for only a little over a $\frac{1}{4}$ the time shown, and Man can hardly be fitted onto the clock face.

rctic Fox; Reindeer.

n Oceans.

untains.

ike reptiles.

Most of the knowledge of early life on Earth has been gained from the study of rocks and fossils which have been buried in the various strata (layers) of rock.

Fossils are the remains or traces of things that lived in ancient times and were buried in the various layers of rock that built up over hundreds of thousands of years.

DISCOVERING PREHISTORY

Q. ARE ANCIENT BEINGS DISCOURSING PALAEONTOLOGISTS?

- **Palaeontology** is t[h]e name given to the study of fossils an[d] prehistoric life. This word is made up from 3 Greek words: **'palaios'** – **'ancient'**; **'onta'** – **'beings'** and **'logos** '**discourse'** (discussion).

- The word **'fossil'** is taken from a Latin word **'fossilis'** which means **'something dug up'**.

- In the famous **tar pits** in North America, skeletons of prehistoric animals have been **preserved**. The animals had become **stuck** in the bogs and preserved in the sediment at the bottom.

- The **first record** of the discovery of a dinosaur bone is of one found in a quarry in Cornwall in **1677**.

- **100,000** different species of extinct animals have been discovered by palaeontologists.

2 POUNDS OF FROZEN MAMMOTH, PLEASE

Woolly Mammoths

- **Deep-frozen** mammoths have been found in the snow in Siberia. They were so **well preserved** that when allowed to thaw, they **still** had blood in their bodies and dogs were able to **eat** the flesh that was **thousands** of years old.

FROZEN MAMMOTH

- Many insects and small animals are **embedded** in **amber**. Amber was originally the **resin** which oozed from prehistoric pine trees. Insects, flowers feathers and small animals became **stuck** in the resin which covered them. The resin hardened to amber and preserved what was trapped in it.

The **first** fossil **ichthyosaur** was found in Lyme Regis, England, in the early 19th century. It was found by Mary Anning when she was 11, and she grew up to become a great fossil expert.

Iguanodon were first assembled in the **wrong** way. The experts had it standing on all **4** legs, with its pointed thumb sticking out of its **forehead** like a horn!

Years later it was discovered that it walked on its **2** back legs, and the pointed horn was attached to its hand.

31 Iguanodon were found in a Belgian coal-mine in **1878**.

Iguanodon

Many prehistoric mammoths were reconstructed with their tusks the **wrong** way round. The experts thought they used them for attack and had them pointing **out**. They had to be **swapped** when it was found the tusks curved **in** towards each other.

There is a town called **Dinosaur** in the State of Colorado, U.S.A. Some of the streets are named after different types of dinosaurs, like **Allosaurus Avenue** and **Trachodon Terrace**.

The finding of **shark's** teeth on **dry** land started a **whole new theory** on how land was formed. Nicolaus Steno, a Danish scientist, believed rock strata was layed down in a **successive** series. The fish's teeth on land showed that at one time the land (Malta) had been covered by sea.

The 1st Roman Emperor, Augustus Caesar, **decorated** his palace with fossils.

The early fossil finders thought that the animals they were finding were the ones that drowned in **Noah's** flood.

IS THERE ROOM FOR US IN THERE?

EARLY LIFE

Conditions which were suitable for the generation of life first existed about **3,300 million** years ago.

The **first** events in the creation of life took place in **Pre-Cambrian** seas. After centuries of rain, the Earth cooled and vast oceans were formed.

The **oldest** preserved organisms known to man are **bacteria** and very simple **blue-green algae**, which have been found in South Africa in rocks estimated to be **3,200 million** years old.

570 million years ago there were no trees, no grass, no shrubs, and no living things on the barren land. Life existed **only** in the sea.

Jellyfish

By the close of the Pre-Cambrian period one important animal must have appeared. This was the ancestor of the sea-urchins and star-fishes, which gave rise to the group of animals to which **vertebrates** (animals with backbones) belong.

Mollusks

Ancestor of the Sea-Urchin

Brachiopods

About **30%** of the animal fossils found in Cambrian rocks are **Brachiopods**, small 'shellfish'.

The simple marine life which has been found as fossils have to be magnified over **300 times**.

Fossils from the **Pre-Cambrian period** are very **rare** because the forms of life were simple and very small.

The **simplest** living things can often adapt and survive best. For example, **Sponges** are almost unchanged after **600 million** years, and **Jellyfish** swam through the seas then as they do today.

Sponges

All the main groups of animals, except the vertebrates, had appeared by the beginning of the Cambrian period. Up until now, **500** individual species have been identified.

Nautiloids

60% of the animals living in the **Palaeozoic** era were **Trilobites**. They belong to the group **Arthropods** which includes crabs, insects, centipedes, spiders and shrimps. Trilobites carried a skeleton on the **outside** of their bodies. The largest was **Paradoxides**, about 30.5 inches, though they were usually **0.4-1 inch**.

The **first** meat-eaters that ruled the seas were **Nautiloids**, impressive Ordovician animals. They looked like squid surrounded by a horn-shaped shell and the largest grew to **14.75 feet**.

Corals first appeared in the **Ordovician** seas. They built reefs, like the corals today.

Corals

Colors are rarely preserved, but clear bands of maroon have remained imprinted in a fossilized **Brachiopod** over **350 million** years old.

Mollusks, the group which includes slugs, snails, oysters and octupi are common **Cambrian** fossils which you can still see on beaches today.

Trilobites

Groups of animals that have adapted to one environment often produce members which **change back** to the environment in which they **previously** lived.

Several reptiles, like **Ichthyosaurs**, **Plesiosaurs** and **Pliosaurs**, adapted to living in the **sea** at a time when reptiles were **masters** of the **land** and **air**.

225 million years ago **Plesiosaurs** appeared. Their limbs were transformed to **swimming fins**, and they had short bodies, flattened underneath.

There were **2** types of Plesiosaurs: **long**-necked and **short**-necked. Some long-necked Plesiosaurs had **76** vertebrae, while short-necked ones had about **13**.

Short-necked Plesiosaur

The **Dinichtys**, 'terrible fish', grew to a length of **20 feet**, $\frac{1}{3}$ of which was its armored head.

Duncleostus was an enormous, **34.5 feet**, **Placoderm**.

Placoderm

The shark, **Pleuracanthus**, had a spine which **stuck out** at the back of its head, lined with **teeth-like** points. Its skeleton was cartilage and it was about **28.4 inches** long.

Sharks, like this, ruled the **Carboniferou** waters.

Dinichtys

Placoderms 'plate-skinned', were the first fish with **jaws**. Unlike Agnatha they had **paired limbs**. This meant Placoderms could **eat new types** of food, which eventually allowed their descendants to **move from** the water to land.

Agnatha

Agnatha were the m primitive fish. Many had heavy, bony sca covering them. The modern **hag-fish** an **lamprey** are the only Agnatha that surviv

Trilobites

Plesiosaurs may have been able to **crawl** on the seashore, as **seals** do, as their undersides were protected with strong ribs and their wide, paddle-like limbs could drag them along.

Long-necked Plesiosaur

Plesiosaurs 32½ feet long swam over Australia. The neck of **Elasmosaurus**, found in America, was **28 feet**, with **76** vertebrae.

Lungs may have been developed by fresh-water fish in the **Devonian** Period, when there seem to have been **droughts**. Lungs enabled them to absorb **oxygen** directly from the atmosphere.

By the end of the **Devonian** Period the **largest** group of fresh-water vertebrates were **bony fish** about **4 inches** long.

There are **2** groups of bony fish: '**ray-finned**' and the '**nostril**' fish.

All land-dwelling mammals, **including Man**, developed from '**nostril**' fish.

250 million years ago 'ray-finned' fish **moved** from fresh-water **to the sea**. They are **now 90%** of living fish.

Ichthyosaurs, 'fish lizard', had up to **200** teeth, and as many as **200** vertebrae, $\frac{2}{3}$ of which were in their **tail**. They looked like dolphins, were about **7 feet** long, and lived in the **Mesozoic** seas.

Ichthyosaur

As an **Ichthyosaur** grew **older** its head **decreased** in size in proportion to the rest of its body.

Pleuracanthus

Leptopterygius acutirostris was the **largest** Icthyosaur. Its skull was **7 feet** long; its overall length was **43 feet**; and its largest vertebrae were **8 inches** across. These giants lived in the **Jurassic** Period.

Jawless, fish-like animals called **Ostracoderms** 'shell-skinned' are the **earliest vertebrates** found so far. They were in rocks **500 million** years old.

For **400 million** years **King crabs** have remained virtually **unchanged**.

Nautiloids

King crab

AMPHIBIANS

Amphibians take their name from 2 Greek words: 'Amphi' means 'both kinds' and 'bios' means 'life'. They are called **amphibians** because of their ability to live **both in water and on land**.

The **transition** from fish to amphibian is not fully understood, but it is likely that as the Earth's water supply began to dry out many fish had to find a new home or die. The fish who had stronger fins and who could breathe out of water were able to crawl to new pools of water when their old habitats dried out. As this process continued, the fins grew stronger, until they could really be called '**limbs**'.

The first amphibians still needed **water** to survive. They needed water to **hatch** their eggs. Their main **source of food** was in the sea, and they hadn't found a way to stop the loss of their body fluid through evaporation.

Amphibians **still** lay their eggs in water. Many still walk awkwardly on land, their bodies moving from side to side twisting like their fish ancestors.

Ichtyostega

The **oldest** amphibian known is **Ichtyostega**, which had legs and feet but **still** had a **fish's tail**.

Synouria

The **Synouria** is a puzzling animal. Experts cannot decide whether it is an amphibian or a reptile and it is probably a **link** between the two.

Turtle

Turtles probably developed from fresh water amphibians.

The **largest** prehistoric turtle lived during the **Cretaceous Period**. Its shell was about $7\frac{1}{2}$ **feet** and it was about $10\frac{1}{2}$ **feet** long.

Eryops was a huge meat-eater living in the **Permian Period**. It had a large head lined with sharp teeth and could be **6 feet** long.

The **largest** amphibian that ever lived was **Mastadonorous**, in the **Triassic Period**. It seems to have spent most of its time in water, feeding on fish. It was a frightening creature with a skull **3 feet** long.

Amphibians and **reptiles** lived side by side through the early part of the **Permian Period**. After this time there were great **geological changes**. The continental land masses went through great upheavals, which **caused** changes in the climate.

The almost constant humidity which had lasted for thousands of years gave way to **seasonal changes** of wet and dry periods which led to a **decline** in the supremacy of the amphibians.

e important ange from the h-like state s the **reversal** functions of e limbs and tail. ish moves by eans of its tail, th the fins lping to balance. the amphibian, e limbs (once the s) are used for ovement, and the l for balance.

Amphibians were the **most important** animals living on land for **80 million** years.

Amphibians are the **most primitive** land vertebrates.

Eryops

Pteroplax had almost **no limbs** at all, and was about **15 feet** long. It looked rather like a snake, and probably spent most of its time in water.

Pteroplax

The **only** fossil record of the earliest amphibian is **one footprint** made in mud during the **Devonian Period**.

Frog

oday, the largest turtle is the acific Leather-back Turtle hich grows up to **6 feet**.

Frogs and **newts** have lived on Earth for **150 million** years.

Crocodiles developed from the order of reptiles called **Pseudosuchians**. This means that Ichthyosaurs and Plesiosaurs were the **ancestors** of alligators and crocodiles, and that dinosaurs and the flying reptiles, like Pterosaurs, were their **cousins**.

The **best-known** crocodile **ancestor** was the 'socket-toothed' reptile, **Protocuchus**. It lived in N. America and Europe during the **Triassic** and early **Jurassic** Period.

ALLIGATORS,

An early crocodile was **Steneosaurus bollensis**. It grew as long as **20 feet**. It had **4** limbs with webbed feet; with **4** toes on its back feet and **5** toes on its front feet. The first **3** toes of each foot had sharp claws.

One so-called 'mammalian reptile' which lived in the late **Carboniferous** and early **Permian** Period was **Dimetrodon**. This fierce meat-eater had **2** types of teeth. At the front of its mouth were dagger-like teeth for stabbing its prey. The sides were lined with shorter teeth that cut the food and chewed it.

The '**fin**' was made from **skin** stretched over vertical spines.

Phytosaurs, which looked like crocodiles, lived **30 million** years **before** real crocod appeared.

The fin may have helped **camouflage** the reptile, or it may have helped **regulate** its body temperature. It may have been a '**heating pad**' catching the sunlight, or used as a **fan**.

Several reptiles, including **Dimetrodon**, had a '**fin**' which grew out of the top of its back.

Some **Phytosaurs** from N. America had skulls as long as **4 feet**.

Many of the 'ruling reptiles', including dinosaurs, were able to hunt their prey by **standing** and **running** on their 2 back legs.

Dimetrodon

This left their front limbs free to act as **primitive arms**.

During the **Cretaceous Period** the biggest crocodiles may have preyed on the dinosaurs.

ROCODILES AND MEAT-EATING REPTILES

The **largest** prehistoric crocodile was found in Montana, N. America. It was called **Phobosuchus hatcheri** and was **50 feet** long. Other specimens probably grew **even** longer.

Geosaurs reverted to living **entirely in the sea**. They developed a smooth skin; their limbs were transformed into fins, and their tail became shaped like a fish's tail.

2 marine crocodiles were the size of large fish. **Alligathrium** was only **16.3 inches** and **Alligatorellus** was **9.2 inches** from nose to tail.

Phytosaur

A **Phytosaur's** nostrils were on its **forehead**, just **above** its eyes.

In a **crocodile**, the nostrils are down on the end of its **muzzle**.

Neither prehistoric nor modern crocodiles are able to **stick out their tongues**.

The **'family'** relation-ship between crocodiles and dinosaurs has enabled zoologists to estimate **how** dinosaurs lived.

Phytosaurs had as many as 300 sharp teeth and were over **20 feet** long.

Eusachian

Modern alligators and crocodiles are descended from the **most** advanced crocodilians called **Eusachians**, which lived in the **Cretaceous** Period.

Pterosaur

Fossilised Pterosaurs have been found in Triassic rocks. They lived about **100 million** years before dying out at the end of the **Cretaceous Period.**

The first animals to conquer the **air** were **flying reptiles** or **Pterosaurs**.

Long-tailed Pterosaurs **died out earlier** than short-tailed ones.

Rhamphorhyncus

Rhamphorhyncus 'beak-snouted' had a short body, about **20 inches**, and a diamond-shaped flap of skin at the end of a long tail.

Different sized teeth that pointed forwards filled its large mouth.

Scientists believe Pterosaurs **rested** like bats do. They hung upside down gripping the branches with the claws of their stunted back legs.

Pterodactyls had short tails. They lived in flocks and fed on fish and insects in the late Jurassic skies.

There were groups of **Pterosaurs**: **long-tailed,** which had long, pointed heads and jaws with well-developed teeth; and **short-tailed,** which had slender heads, delicate or no teeth, and the tails had become stubs.

Pterosaurs' **wings** were created out of the **2 front limbs** being **covered with skin.** The first **3** fingers had become claws; the **4th** finger had grown very long to support the wing skin; the **5th** finger had **disappeared.**

Pteranodon's body was the size of a turkey, but its wing span was **20 feet.**

The greatest number of **teeth** found in a flying reptile is **360**, which were arranged like a comb in the mouth of **Ctenochasma**.

Although many Pterosaurs were very large, they had **hollow** bone and were not heavy.

Birds appeared about the same time as flying reptiles, but they developed from a totally **different** group. Their only common feature was that they could **both** fly.

Archaeopteryx

The **earliest** primitive bird was **Archaeopteryx**. It has **3** clawed toes on each wing, a long tail and scaly jaws armed with teeth, but its body and wings were **covered with feathers.**

FLYING CREATURES

Quetzalcoatlus was discovered in Texas in 1975. It is the **largest flying** creature known, and was a vulture-like, soaring Pterosaur.

The **largest** prehistoric **insect** was a **dragonfly** in the **Permian Period**. Its wing span was over **28 inches**.

Today, the largest dragon-fly lives in Central and South America and has a wing span of only **7.6 inches**.

Beetles, crickets, butterflies and wasps evolved in the **Permian Period**.

One major question that has baffled zoologists, is, **how** flying reptiles flew?

The answer probably lies **buried** in rock waiting to be found.

Some experts think they used their claws to **climb** trees, and then glided. Others think they may have **fluttered** to the right height and then glided. It may be that flying reptiles were **not** as cold-blooded as we think. Perhaps they had a means of maintaining their body heat which enabled them to produce the energy to fly.

The **only mammals** able to fly are **bats**. The earliest bats appeared in the **Eocene Period**, and were hardly different from bats today. Their ancestors must have lived earlier.

Feathers meant Archaeopteryx could maintain a **constant** body temperature. They **insulated** the body retaining the heat, creating a warm-blooded system. Feathers improved flying and were stronger and more efficient than skin wings.

Gigantornis eaglesomi was the **largest** bird in the **Eocene Period**. Its wing span was **20 feet**.

The wing span of the Wandering Albatross, the largest bird today, is **half** this width.

PREHISTORIC BIRDS THAT COULD NOT FLY

The **Elephant Bird** was the **largest** prehistoric bird. It was over **9.84 feet** high and weighed about **100 pounds**.

It laid the **largest** egg ever known with a capacity of **9.41 quarts**, **7** times the size of an ostrich egg. You can make an omelette for **12** people with an ostrich egg. You could make one for **84** people with an Elephant Bird egg.

EGG STALL

1 EGG FOR 6 SKINS

Eurapteryx was a member of the **emu** family. It had very powerful legs and a huge body, which made its blunt skull and short, wide beak look very peculiar.

One member of the species called **Eurapteryx elephantopus**, 'elephant footed', had huge clawed feet.

Diatryma was a meat-eating bird of the **Eocene Period** which lived on the grasslands of N. America and Euro[pe]

The **moas**, the flightless birds of New Zealand, had strong skeletons, powerful legs, and small skulls with short, flat beaks.

By the 18th century they had been hunted to extinction by the Maoris who lived on the island.

Many of the flightless birds of S. America lived lives very **like** the **flesh-eating** mammals.

Phororacus lived **15 million** years ago. It had a skull as large as a **horse**, stood **9.84 feet** high and devoured its prey with a great, hooked beak and savage claws.

It had a great head, **18 inches** long, and a stron[g] hooked beak with which it attacked and ate its prey. Its neck and body were strong, and its powerful runnings legs ended in **4** toes on each foot.

Phororacus

Diatryma

SNAKES AND LIZARDS

The ancestors of **snakes** and **lizards** evolved during the **Triassic Period** and are grouped under the name **Squamata**. All of the **2,500** species of lizards and the same number of snake species that we know today, developed from these Triassic ancestors.

Many zoologists believe that snakes developed from **burrowing lizards** that had **lost** their digging limbs.

The snakes that first appeared in the the **Cretaceous Period** would **still** be recognizable as snakes today.

Modern **boas** and **pythons** have changed very little over the past **100 million** years.

Poisonous snakes only developed during the **Cenozoic** era, and so are only **half** the age of the other snakes.

Snake fossils are extremely **rare** because a snake's skeleton is **very delicate**.

Rainbow Boa

The **most primitive living** reptile is the **Tuatara**. It is the **last** survivor of a prehistoric reptile group called **Rhyncocephalia**.

It used to live throughout the world, but now is only found in New Zealand.

The Tuatara only comes out into the open at night from its burrow to hunt insects and small animals. It takes **20 years** to become an adult. Its eggs take **15 months** before they hatch.

There are **still** prehistoric lizards living on the island of Komodo, Indonesia. These **Komodo monitors** can grow up to **9.8 feet** and weigh **100 pounds**. They are the **largest** of all living lizards.

The **longest** prehistoric snake looked like a modern python. It was called **Gigantophis garstini.** Fossil remains have led experts to estimate its length at about **37 feet**.

Tylosaurus was a meat-eating lizard living in the **Upper Cretaceous Period**. It grew to **30 feet** in length.

Mosasaurs were ferocious giants with a savage **temper**. They killed and ate large, dangerous fish like **Portheus**, which was **9.84 feet**, and they also attacked each other.

Many were over **39.36 feet** long, half of which was a long, powerful tail for swimming.

group of sea-lizards, asaur, evolved and out within the taceous Period. ir history only ed **30 million** years.

Mosasaur

The spine of a Mosasaur had **130** vertebrae.

You can tell the difference between a dinosaur and a reptile by looking at their **legs**. The dinosaur's limbs were **underneath** its body with knees pointing forwards and elbows backwards. Movement was quicker and easier than for reptiles who had to **crawl** on their stomachs because theirs legs were on the **side** of their bodies.

Plateosaurus

Allosaur

Dinosaur bones are much **heavier** and **stronger** than the similar bones in mammals.

Dinosaurs are divided into **2** groups according to the **shape** of their hip bones: 'bird-hipped' and 'lizard-hipped'.

Many of the 'bird-hipped' dinosaurs were **2-legged**, though some of the later ones went back to moving on 4 legs.

'Lizard-hipped' dinosaurs could be either 2 or 4 legged.

It is possible that dinosaurs had **color** vision. Lizards, turtles and tortoises have color vision, and as they are related to dinosaurs, dinosaurs probably could see color as well.

Meat-eating dinosaurs of all sizes ran about on their **back legs**.

One of the **largest** meat-eaters was **Allosaurus**, which grew over **32.8 feet** long. It ran on 2 strong back legs using its tail to balance. Its head was large and its mouth contained rows of vicious teeth. Each foot had **3** sharp claws.

The world in which dinosaurs developed was ruled by many different types of **reptiles**. The dinosaurs soon established their supremacy and for about **120 million years ruled the world. No other** group of animals, including Man, has ruled for so long.

Some experts think that dinosaurs may have been **incapable of thinking**.

The brain cavity in fossilized skulls has led them to say that a dinosaur's actions are reactions to the senses like smell, sight and hearing. They are 'instinctive reactions' which happen **automatically** and do not involve thinking.

The **heaviest** animal that lived on land was **Brachiosaurus**. It grew to **41.7 feet** and weighed **78.26 tons**. Its front legs were **longer** than the back ones. Its eyes and nostrils were **high** on its head so it could almost disappear under water if in danger and **still** breathe and see.

The **largest** 2-legged dinosaur that ever lived was the savage meat-eater **Tyrannosaurus Rex**. It had huge jaws with dagger-like teeth, some **6 inches** long. It had short stumpy arms that could not reach its mouth.

Tyrannosaurus Rex

The **earliest** dinosaurs were small, agile creatures only about **3.28 feet** long. They ran about on their **back legs** and were quick and nimble.

Fossilized footprints of Tyrannosaurus are nearly **28.8 in** long and **31.6 inc** wide, and the distance of the animal's stride was **12½ feet**.

DINOSAURS

The name **Dinosaur** was given to these prehistoric reptiles in 1841. It is made up of 2 Greek words: '**deinos**' which means '**terrible**' and '**sauros**' which means '**lizard**'.

The skulls of dinosaurs are **small** in proportion to the rest of their bodies.

Brachiosaurus

Apatosaurus, which means 'unreal lizard' is the correct name for **Brontosaurus** 'thunder lizard'. It weighed about **20 tons** and grew to a length of **60 feet**. It ate the soft plants that grew in the marshes.

The tiny head of Apatosaurus was the **same** width as its neck. Its brain only weighed **1 pound** and was used to work its jaws and provide a warning system in case of danger. The muscles which operated its back legs were controlled by a bulge in the nervous system at the base of its spine.

Diplodocus

Coelophysis

One of the largest dinosaurs discovered is **Diplodocus**, who grew to a length of **$87\frac{1}{2}$ feet**, almost the length of **3** double decker buses.

Coelophysis was one of the earliest dinosaurs, and was only **9.84 feet** long. It was a **meat-eater** with 3 sharp claws on its hands and feet and long jaws filled with razor-sharp teeth.

Ankylosaurus was covered with **armor**. Its back was protected by curved plates; its head was covered by a bone helmet; long, bony spikes shielded its legs and its tail was covered with rings of bone and ended with a great bone club.

Triceratops

The **largest horned** dinosaur was **Triceratops** 'three-horned lizard'.
Height: 8 feet
Length: 20 feet
Skull: 7 feet.

Ankylosaurus

Many of the **plant**-eating dinosaurs grew **very large** and **heavy**, and had to move on all **4** legs.

Diplodocus

Ceratosaurus, 'horned lizard', had a large outcrop of bone on its nose. It was a vicious meat-eater, about $16\frac{1}{2}$ **feet** long. Its **8** fingers had sharp claws, and its mouth was lined with jagged teeth.

Megalosaurus

Ceratosaurus

The first dinosaur to be given a name was **Megalosaurus**, 'large lizard', in 1824.

Protoceratops was the **first** of the large family of **horn-faced** dinosaurs. It had a large skull which ended in a hooked beak. A frill or collar of bone projected from the back of the skull, sticking out over its neck.

Fossils show that **newly hatched** Protoceratops did **not** have this frill, so it must have **developed** as the animal grew.

After living on Earth for **100 million** years the dinosaurs suddenly **disappear** at the end of the **Cretaceous Period**.

A **change** in the climate may have killed them off. A '**dinosaur plague**' may have been responsible. Perhaps it was the growing group of **egg-eating** mammals that prevented the hatching of young dinosaurs. **Nobody** really knows why they disappeared.

Styracosaurus had a huge horn **6 feet** long and **2 feet** round, which stuck out from its nose.

Corythosaurus had a hollow horn on top of its head which may have **increased** its **sense of smell**.

Ankylosaurus

Corythosaurus

DINOSAURS

Spinosaurus 'spine lizard' was one of the **fiercest** dinosaurs of the **Lower Cretaceous Period**. It had an extraordinary **fin** growing out of its back, supported by spines that were up to $6\frac{1}{2}$ **feet** long.

Stegosaurus

Iguanodon was named after its **tooth** was discovered in 1825 and **mistaken** for the tooth of an Iguana.

It lived on plants, and its teeth were constantly being **worn down**. Its main means of defence were its sharp, pointed thumbs.

Stegosaurus is called the **most brainless** prehistoric animal. Its **tiny brain** was the size of a **walnut** and weighed **2.45 ounces** which was **0.004%** of its total body weight.

Height: 15 feet
Length: 30 feet
Weight: 3-4 tons.

Iguanodon

100,000,000 YEAR OLD BIRTHDAY

Spinosaurus

Poleocanthus

Styracosaurus

Poleocanthus walked on all fours and was protected by **armour plating**.

Mammals are **different** from other animal groups in the following ways:
  *they are **vertebrates** (have a spinal column)
  *they have **warm** blood and are covered with **hair**
  *the young mammals start life by **drinking their mother's milk**.

Mammals are divided into **2** groups depending on the way they give birth to their young:

1. Marsupials – like possums and kangaroos, produce very **under-developed** young, which after they are born, live **in** their mother's pouch, where they feed on their mother's milk while they grow and develop enough to survive on their own outside.

2. Placental mammals – give birth to far **more advanced** young who already have **all** the main body features. They live **outside** the mother and are fed on her milk when young.

The **shape** of the Earth **changed** greatly at the end of the **Cretaceous Period**. The Alps, Pyrenees and Himalayas were **completed**. Their construction and volcanic activity **changed the climate**. This affected the habitats of **all** the animals.

Many different animals evolved as they adapted to the **new** environments.

Mammalian features appeared in some **reptiles** in the **Triassic Period**. They developed dog-like skulls and teeth of **different** types.

Cynognathus, a reptile **7 feet** long, showed these features. It also had its feet **underneath** its body, not at the side.

By the **Paleocene Period** there were **400** species of mammals.

The **first** mammal young were probably **hatched** from **eggs**. The platypus is **still** hatched from an egg.

Marsupial

Placental

Platypus

For their first **80 million** years, mammals stayed **small**, possibly to avoid the meat-eating dinosaurs who wanted larger prey.

Animals with **hooves** are called **ungulates**, and they evolved in the **Palaeocene Period**. There are **2** groups:
Odd-toed: like horses, rhinoceroses, where the **central** toe provides the **main** support and is the **strongest** toe.
Even-toed: like pigs and camels, which have **2** equally developed toes which share the body weight.

Notharctus lived in forests and lived off fruit and insects. It grew to an overall length of about **3.28 feet**, half of which was tail. Its face was thin, like a fox's, and it had large eyes. It could use its toes to grasp things, like we use our fingers. Notharctus was one of the ancestors of the first primates – the group to which human beings belong.

The only mammals that have ever mastered the art of **flying** are **bats**. These first appeared in the Eocene period and resembled the long extinct Pterosaurus in the structure of their wings.

The **earliest primates** looked like modern lemurs. There were 3 main groups. The **flat-nosed monkeys** of the New World, lived in S. America; the **narrow-nosed monkeys** of the Old World lived in Europe and Asia and gave rise to the **third** group, the **Hominoidea**, at the end of the **Oligocene Period**. This new group included all the **anthropoid** (**man-like**) apes, chimpanzees, gorillas and early man.

Cats descended from weasel-like animals. They were divided into **2** groups. **Biting** cats were called **Dinictis** and those cats that **stabbed** their prey were called **Hoplophoneus**.

largest 'stabbing cat'
Smilodon, the Sabre-
[toot]hed tiger. It was
[fat]ter than a modern
[cat] but built more heavily.
[u]pper jaws had 2 pointed
[tusk]s, 9.2 inches long, with
[whi]ch it stabbed its prey.
[whe]n it opened its
[mou]th its lower jaw pointed
[str]aight down and didn't get
[in th]e way of the long
[uppe]r teeth. It was
[able] to breathe even when
[its n]ose was buried in its
[victi]m, because its nostrils
[wer]e set back from the
[end] of its muzzle.

Ceratogaulus was a
rodent 2 feet long.
It is called 'horned
digger' because of the
pair of sharp horns
in the middle of its
forehead. Nobody knows
what these horns
were used for.

Pheodocus was about
the size of a sheep.
As well as big canine
teeth it had a series
of teeth lining its
cheeks to help it grind
plant food.

The first placentals
must have returned to
the sea in the
Palaeocene Period,
because sea-cows and
large whales were
already well developed
by the Eocene Period.

Like the reptiles
before them, some
mammals returned to
the water and adapted
their walking limbs
to swimming organs.

One of the strangest
looking mammals was
Glyptodont, which
resembles Stegosaurus
from the dinosaur
period of millions
of years before.
Glyptodont was
covered in armor
plating. It measured
14 feet long and
5.5 feet high. The end
of its tail is perhaps
the most curious
feature as it was
covered with a growth
of bony spikes like a
medieval weapon.

PRE-HISTORIC MAMMALIAN ZOO

The largest
prehistoric whale
was Basilosaurus.
It was about 65.6
feet of which
5 feet was head,
9.84 feet was body
and the rest tail.
It weighed about
17 tons.

MAMMALS

BRONTOTHERIUM

Moropus was a peculiar looking animal, like a cross between a camel, a bear and a horse.

Moropus was about the size of a horse, with long limbs, a deep face and a compact body. Its front legs were **longer** than its back ones, and instead of hooves, it had **claws** on the end of its **3 toes**.

Brontotherium became extinct because it could not adapt to a **changing environment**. This huge beast was **15 feet** long and **8 feet** high, and had a large, flat horn made of bone. It fed on **soft** plants and did not develop teeth strong enough to eat the new tougher grass starting to grow on the plains where it grazed.

MOROPUS

Uintatherium was the **largest** animal living in the **Palaeocene Period**. It was **11.97 feet** long and **7 feet** high at the shoulder. The 6 horns on its skull were large **outcrops** covered with skin. Its skull was over **3.28 feet** long. Uintatherium weighed **4-5 tons**.

UI

CAMEL RIDES HERE

Camels began life in N. America, though they have been extinct there for thousands of years.

One of the largest of the strange creatures that appeared in South America was a **giant sloth**, Megatherium. It was the size of an elephant, and walked on the **sides** of its feet because of the curved claws that grew at the end of each foot. It fed on leaves on the upper branches which it reached by rearing up on its back legs to a height of **18 feet**.

lmost all mammals rew to their **largest** ze during the liocene Period.

MEGATHERIUM

Until only **50,000** years ago, a **giant deer**, with antlers that spread almost **8.2 feet**, lived on Earth. These antlers could weigh from **100-132 pounds**. This deer is sometimes called the **Irish elk**.

Castoroides was a huge **beaver** with a **7 feet** body and a long tail. It could probably gnaw down the largest trees with ease.

The **largest land** animal **ever** recorded was a hornless rhinoceros, **Baluchitherium**, which lived in the **Oligocene Period**. Its head was **4.92 feet** long; the neck was **5.97 feet** long, the body **15.97 feet** long. It stood **18.04 feet** high at the shoulder. The gap underneath its belly was wide enough for **6 people** to march side by side. It was **tall** enough to look over a **2 storey** house and it weighed **16-20 tons**.

THERIUM

BALUCHITHERIUM

Until the **Eocene Period** most mammals were small, but at this time the first **giant plant-eaters** appeared. One of the biggest was shaped like a barrel and weighed almost **990 pounds**.

These early giants had large bodies, but their brains were **small**. **Uintathere** was as heavy as a modern elephant, but had a smaller brain than a modern rhinoceros.

MAMMOTHS AND MASTODONS

The mammoth's trunk was unusual. Prehistoric cave paintings and preserved trunks found in the frozen areas of Siberia, show a **finger-like projection** sticking out of the upper edge of the trunk and a **wide flap**, like a lip, on the bottom edge. These were probably used to grip small objects.

When the Mediterranean islands, like Malta, were cut off from the mainland early in the Pleistocene period, a type of **pygmy elephant** developed on these islands. One, on Malta, was called **Loxodonta falceroni** and was the size of a pony.

The ancestor of all mammoths and elephants was an animal called **Moeritherium**. It didn't look much like a modern elephant. It had no tusks, no trunk and was about the **size of a pig**. It had one pair of teeth larger than the others and used, probably, for digging up roots.

Because they lived in cold climates **woolly mammoths** were covered with hair. Below their knees this hair was **6-7 inches** long. Above the knee it was **14 inches** long and on its back the hair grew to a length of **16-18 inches**. Under this was a second layer of fine **under hair** which only grew **1-2 inches**. A mammoth's tusks grew **away** from each other and then came together at the tips, forming a shape like the outer edges of a spoon. They usually grew to a length of **9-10 feet** though they sometimes reached the extreme length of **13½ feet**.

Some of the early mastodons had **4 tusks**; 2 in the upper jaw curving down, and 2 in the lower jaw curving up. Later mastodons looked more like elephants. The last mastodons may have lived **10,000 years** ago in N. America.

Mammoths needed to **eat** a lot of food each day – and for most of the year, its food was under snow. It may have used its tusks to clear the snow to find the grass and plants more easily.

Scientists think a mammoth used its tusks to **find food**, as well as for attack.

Moeritherium

Gomphotherium

Dinotheres had tusks which turned in toward its body.

The largest European mammoth was **Palaeoloxodon**. This forest-dwelling mammoth was **15-17 feet** high, and had straight tusks over **9.8 feet** long.

Prehistoric man **hunted** mammoths for food and skins. The **remains** of over **1,000** mammoths have been found at the site of a prehistoric settlement in Czechoslovakia.

In the **warmer** climates of southern Africa and Asia lived a mammal **larger** than the northern ones, and with much **less** hair (in the very warm climates it had almost **no** hair at all).

About 5 million years after Moeritherium had lived, 'ancient mastodon', **Palaemastodon**, appeared. It stood **twice** as high as its ancestor. Its 2 front teeth had flattened out and grown into tusks, and its lower jaw jutted forward too.

The only mammoth carcases that have survived are those of **northern woolly mammoths** that have been frozen solid in the very cold areas of N. Siberia.

Archaeologists in the Ukraine have discovered that early man used mammoth bones as **building materials**. They have found huts built with their shoulder blades, skulls and other long bones. The outer covering of the hut may have been the mammoth's skin.

The mammoth's bones were **bigger** and **stronger** than the bones in elephants, and its skull was **shaped differently**. The mammoth's molar teeth, used for grinding, usually had a number of **enamel ridges**, which an elephant's molars don't have. The mammoth's tusks were **longer** than an elephants, and curved **inwards** to meet each other.

Mastodons split from the ancestors of elephants and mammoths when the mammoths developed a new type of flat-ridged grinding tooth. The mastodon's name means 'nipple tooth'.

Woolly mammoths had a pair of **fatty humps** which were probably used to store fat as an energy reserve to be used in the long, cold winters.

Elephants as we know them today had appeared by the later part of the **Pliocene Period**.

Dinotherium

Mammoth

Indian Elephant

PREHISTORIC ANIMALS

Australian lungfish: this fish was discovered in 1896. Its ancestors first appeared in the **Devonian Period 350 million** years ago and this species is estimated to be **200 million** years old. It takes air into its single lung directly from the atmosphere and forces the used air out of its gullet with a loud grunt.

Australian Lungfish

I HAVE BEEN HERE LONGER THAN ANYONE

Lingula

Lingula: this brachiopod has remained **almost unchanged** since it first appeared in the **Lower Cambrian** seas over **550 million** years ago. It has been on Earth **longer** than any other animal.

Coelacanth

Coelacanth: scientists were given a surprise in 1938 when one of these prehistoric fishes was dredged up off the coast of South Africa. Far from being extinct 70 million years ago, as everyone thought, the Coelacanth was **alive** and **well** and living in the Indian Ocean. Since then several others have been caught. The **first** Coelacanth appeared at the end of the **Silurian Period**, about **400 million** years ago.

Peripatus: is a **500 million** year old worm which is found in the tropics today.

A VERY OLD WORM

Peripatus

The Duck-billed Platypus: is the only mammal, apart from the Echidna, which **lays eggs**. It is the **most primitive** living mammal and its brain is very simple compared with the brains of other mammals. It lives in the fresh waters of S. & E. Australia and Tasmania feeding on small water creatures like insects and worms.

A Duck-billed Platypus can eat **its own weight** in worms in a single day.

It was first recorded in 1797, but it has lived on Earth for at least **150 million** years.

ONE DAYS RATIONS

Duck-billed Platypus

LIVING TODAY

Echidna: is one of the only two mammals that lay eggs. The Echidna is also called the **spiny ant-eater**, because of the covering of thick spines all over its back. Today they only live in rocky parts of Australia and New Zealand, but they were much more widespread **150 million** years ago.

Solenodon: like the Coelacanth and the Lingula, it is sometimes called a **living fossil**, because, by studying it, scientists can get an idea of what the early 'placental' mammals were like.

Solenodon is the same size as a small cat. It has poor eyesight and hearing, and its neck and head are so low it has to walk like a crab, moving from side to side. It has survived for **60 million** years. Today, it is only found on the islands of Cuba and Hispaniola, and is sadly being hunted to the point of extinction.

Solenodon

Stephens Island Frog: it is believed that this amphibian is the **ancestor** of **all** the frogs we know today. It was discovered in New Zealand in 1917, and still lives there. Its estimated age is between **170-275 million** years old. It does **not** have webbed toes like all other living frogs.

Okapi: this shy relative of the giraffe was discovered in 1901. It lives in the densest parts of the tropical forest in Central Africa. It is about the size of a large mule.

SHY OKAPI →

Okapi

Like the giraffe, it eats the leaves of trees using its long tongue. The okapi has remained almost unchanged for **30 million** years.

Stephens Island Frog

Tuatara: today the Tuatara only lives in certain parts of New Zealand.

Tuatara   **200 million** years ago, the group of reptiles of which it is the **last survivor** was **widely distributed** throughout the world.

PRESENT DAY ANIMALS AND THEIR PREHISTORIC ANCESTORS

Aardvark: is the closest living relative of the earliest ungulates (animals with hooves) that appeared in the **Palaeocene Period**.

African elephant: evolved from the prehistoric mammoth, **Palaeoxodon Antiquus**, which may have had straight tusks.

Apes: the first apes developed from monkeys called **Catarrhinae**, which appeared in the **Oligocene Period**. The ancestors of modern apes appeared in the **Miocene** and **Pliocene Periods**.

Bears and dogs: their ancestor is thought to have been **Daphoenodon**. It was about **4.5 feet** long with a wolf-like head, and a cat-like body.

Cats: are descended from a small weasel-like flesh-eater called **Miacis**, which was about the size of a squirrel.

Great White Shark: lived in the **Miocene** seas about **10 million** years ago. It was about $52\frac{1}{2}$ **feet** long, and weighed about **20 tons**.

Horse: evolved from an animal no bigger than a fox-terrier, **Hyracotherium**, 'shrew-beast'. It lived during the **Eocene Period** and had **4 toes** on its front feet and **3 toes** on its back feet.

Rhinoceros: its ancestor was an animal called **Hyracodon** which lived in the **Oligocene Period**. It was about the size of a donkey and had **no horn** on its head.

Tapir: modern tapirs found in S. America and Malaya **still** have **4** front toes and **3** back toes like their ancestors from the **Eocene Period**.

Tortoise and turtle: they first appeared in the **Triassic Period**. One of the oldest was **Proganochelys**, which was about $28\frac{1}{2}$ **inches** long. They have **survived** all the changes.